SHIRE NATURAL HISTORY

THE KESTREL

GORDON RIDDLE

CONTENTS
Introduction 2
Historical review 2
Hunting and feeding 6
The breeding cycle 11
Migration and mortality 19
The future 21
Further reading 24

Cover: *A male kestrel arriving at the nest with a vole.*

Series editor: Jim Flegg.

Copyright © 1990 by Gordon Riddle. First published 1990.
Number 52 in the Shire Natural History series. ISBN 0 7478 0054 5.
All rights reserved. No part of this publication may be reproduced or transmitted in any form or by any means, electronic or mechanical, including photocopy, recording, or any information storage and retrieval system, without permission in writing from the publishers, Shire Publications Ltd, Cromwell House, Church Street, Princes Risborough, Buckinghamshire HP17 9AJ, UK.

Printed in Great Britain by C. I. Thomas & Sons (Haverfordwest) Ltd,
Press Buildings, Merlins Bridge, Haverfordwest, Dyfed SA61 1XF.

Introduction

The kestrel *(Falco tinnunculus)* is one of the commonest birds of prey in Europe. In Britain its estimated breeding population of 70,000 pairs far outnumbers the combined total of all other diurnal raptors. It is a bird of open country, favouring grassland habitats which harbour its main prey species, the short-tailed field vole *(Microtus agrestis)*. Far from being elusive and difficult to watch, the kestrel, with its characteristic hovering hunting technique, is a familiar sight over city wasteland, motorway verge, parkland and pasture. This has resulted in a high-profile relationship with man, a very important factor in the success story of the bird.

Kestrels are normally solitary outside the breeding season but they do form family parties at the end of the summer. Birds also associate in areas where voles are very abundant, when they tolerate close neighbours, and during migration, when they are normally gregarious. Although highly vocal during the breeding season, they are relatively silent throughout the rest of the year.

Small mammals are caught on the ground and the compact body of the kestrel, supported by short sturdy legs, is well suited to cope with the impact caused by a rapid drop on to the prey. In flight the bird has an angular shape due to its long pointed wings; these help to differentiate it from the sparrowhawk *(Accipiter nisus)*, with which it is most often confused and which has more rounded wings.

The kestrel is a medium-sized falcon, typical of many birds of prey in that the sexes are dissimilar in both plumage and size. The female is slightly larger than the male and is consequently heavier, weighing between 154 and 314 grams (5-11 ounces) compared to the male's 136 to 252 grams (5-9 ounces). The kestrel has a wingspan between 71 and 80 cm (28-32 inches), is between 32 and 35 cm long (12-14 inches) and has a tail length of between 12 and 15 cm (5-6 inches). The wings when closed are about 5 cm (2 inches) shorter than the tail.

Both sexes have brown as the dominant body colour, chrome-yellow legs, a grey-blue bill and a dark facial moustache. The head is large, flattened on top, and the shoulders are broad, as in most falcons. However, plumage differences are striking. The attractive, well patterned male is easily distinguished from the drabber female by its grey head and nape, rufous back and buff underparts. The female is more uniform brown but has dark bars on the back and darker, more streaked underparts. Whether in flight or at rest, the most obvious field characteristic to use for separating male from female is the tail pattern. The male has a blue-grey tail with a broad black sub-terminal band and narrow white tip; the tail of the female is brown and regularly barred.

The juvenile kestrel closely resembles the female but is usually paler. However, this is not universal and some young males exhibit strong grey colouring on the tail between the barring. Full adult plumage is not usually attained until the second year but some juveniles will breed in sub-adult plumage.

Historical review

The kestrel has not always been Britain's commonest bird of prey. Before the dense forest cover was greatly reduced by man, the better equipped sparrowhawk and goshawk *(Accipiter gentilis)* were much more numerous and the kestrel must have been restricted in range. By the eleventh century, the opening of the landscape and the emergence of sheep rearing on a huge scale must have provided ideal habitat and prey populations for the kestrel. Deforestation continued throughout medieval times as man's impact on the environment increased, but it was not until the sport of falconry was surpassed in popularity by hunting with the gun that birds of prey began to be severely persecuted by man.

Because of its lowly status in the falconry hierarchy the kestrel probably did not suffer too badly during medieval times. However, in the nineteenth century all birds of prey were persecuted. Labelled, along with other predators, as vermin detrimental to game-rearing stocks, the kestrel and other raptors were poisoned, trapped, shot and hung up on gibbets in their thousands. The era when birds of prey were cherished as valuable possessions was over. Many species were reduced in number and range while others, like the osprey *(Pandion haliaetus)* and the goshawk, were eliminated completely from the British Isles in a century of senseless carnage.

The indiscriminate killing continued well into the twentieth century, only the two world wars providing a respite for the beleaguered raptors when many gamekeepers were in the armed forces. Despite persecution, the kestrel was never in danger of following the larger, more specialised species into extinction. Notwithstanding this, the pressure on the kestrel led to a reduction of numbers, although probably less than that suffered by other species, like the peregrine falcon *(Falco peregrinus)* and sparrowhawk, whose natural prey included gamebirds. It was not that keepers were more enlightened, rather that they concentrated their attention on certain target species. The kestrel also had the advantage of being widely distributed throughout the countryside and, as a consequence, there were ample reservoirs of breeding stock to maintain the population at a relatively high level.

The tide began to turn after the First World War when many of the large sporting estates disappeared and fewer people were employed to kill birds of prey. However, despite pressure from conservationists and protective legislation, persecution still exists today.

Extensive use of agricultural pesticides during and after the Second World War resulted in a further decline in the number of birds of prey. Many of the chemicals did not break down easily in the environment and eventually accumulated in the vital organs of avian predators which had fed on contaminated prey such as small rodents and seed-eating birds.

1. The kestrel was not immune to the intense persecution of birds of prey in the nineteenth century.

During the 1950s and 1960s many raptor species, including the kestrel, were badly affected. Breeding was impaired, behavioural abnormalities were recorded and many birds died. The problem was particularly acute in the cereal-growing areas of eastern and south-eastern England. Survey work showed that the kestrel had greatly declined in these areas but fortunately this decline was not uniform throughout Britain. The declines became less marked towards the north and west of Britain. The link between the use of pesticides and the catastrophic collapse of peregrine and sparrowhawk breeding populations was not readily accepted for some time because of the obvious commercial implications but eventually a voluntary ban preceded a legal ban on the use of these persistent pesticides. Bird of prey species recovered gradually during the 1970s but even today it is a recurring problem, albeit to a smaller degree.

Kestrel numbers were probably at a low point in 1963 when the already depleted population was further reduced by the previous severe winter. Since then the kestrel breeding population has been

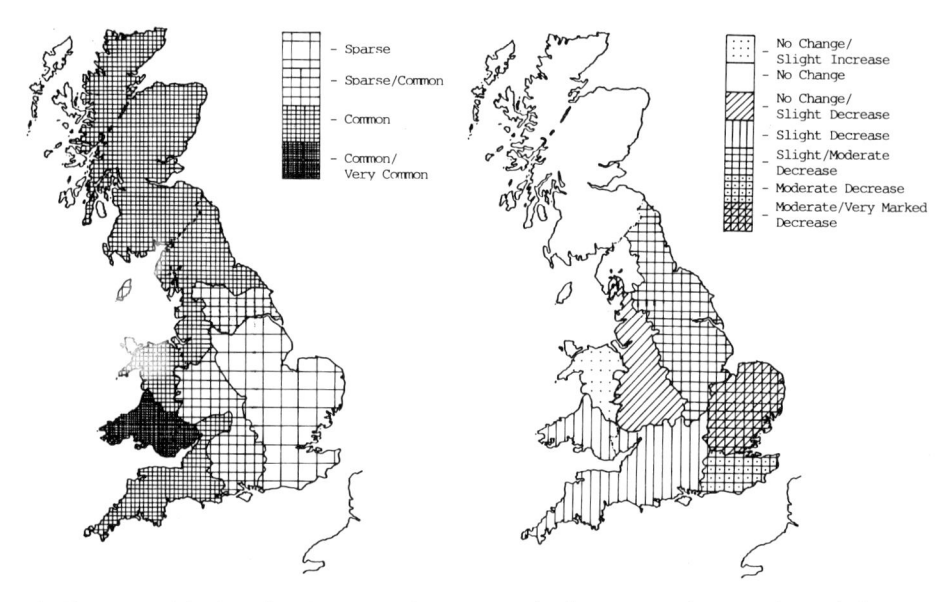

2. *The status of the kestrel in Britain, 1963.*

3. *The fieldwork for the 'Atlas of Breeding Birds in Britain', 1976, recorded kestrels in 92 per cent of 10 km squares.*

on the increase and research carried out between 1968 and 1978 indicated a fivefold increase in breeding pairs, and an increase in the range of habitats used by kestrels. The fieldwork for the *Atlas of Breeding Birds in Britain*, published in 1976, recorded kestrels in 92 per cent of 10 km squares. Apart from Shetland, where the bird was absent as a breeding species, and low numbers in the Fen Country in England and in some areas of the western Highlands of Scotland, the kestrel population seemed to be in excellent health.

There have been two very important trends since the 1960s: firstly, an increase in the colonisation of urban areas, and, secondly, high-density breeding in newly planted upland spruce forests. The bulk of this planting took place in the 1960s and early 1970s when huge tracts of upland sheep pasture and moorland were ploughed, fertilised and planted. The improvement in the quality of upland grassland provided excellent habitat for voles and, in the first six to seven years before the tree canopy closes, there is an abundance of food for kestrels, short-eared owls *(Asio flavineus)*, barn owls *(Tyto alba)* and long-eared owls *(Asio otus)*.

4. Close-up of a hen kestrel showing the notched beak and facial moustache.
5. The characteristic hovering method of hunting is used more in the summer months than in the winter.

In 1984 Ian Newton assessed the kestrel breeding population at an estimated 70,000 pairs and stated that in many parts of Britain the species was close to optimum levels. However, the kestrel is not the commonest raptor in all areas of Britain. In many districts in the west Highlands of Scotland the buzzard *(Buteo buteo)* is more abundant and in well wooded areas, such as Dumfriesshire, the sparrowhawk breeds in much higher density than the kestrel.

The European kestrel has an impressive distribution, being the most abundant diurnal raptor over much of the western Palearctic. From latitude 68 to 70 degrees north it ranges southwards over three continents, Europe, Asia and Africa. There is little evidence of marked changes in the kestrel's range in Europe due to persecution and pesticides but the population sizes vary considerably from country to country. In some countries it is not even the commonest raptor. The lesser kestrel *(Falco naumanni)* is more numerous than the European kestrel in Spain and Greece, while the buzzard outnumbers it in East Germany. The majority of countries have either a stable or an expanding kestrel population following the declines during the pesticide period. However, in nine countries numbers are still falling. Partial or total protective legislation exists in most countries but killing in the name of sport is still prevalent in, for example, Italy, France and Germany. The birds are particularly vulnerable at strategic points on migratory routes such as Malta, where the death toll is severe. Britain has far more breeding pairs of kestrels than any other country, with Spain coming in second place with 30,000 pairs.

Hunting and feeding

The kestrel is most often portrayed in a hovering pose, above grassland, hunting its favourite prey, the short-tailed field vole. However, the kestrel exploits a variety of different prey species and uses a range of hunting techniques depending upon the season, prey availability, prevailing ground cover and weather conditions. It is an opportunist capable of hunting in poor light conditions at dawn and dusk, and it has even been recorded hovering by the illumination of motorway lights and by moonlight. In Northern Ireland and the Isle of Man, where voles do not occur, the chiefly nocturnal wood mouse *(Apodemus sylvaticus)* is the main prey item and the kestrel is crepuscular by necessity.

The kestrel's hunting techniques are divided into flight hunting and perch hunting from a vantage point. Flight hunting can take two main forms: hovering and soaring. The characteristic hovering, or hanging motionless on an updraught, is used primarily for hunting small mammals, invertebrates, lizards and frogs. Hovering is in effect aerial perching. The strategy is to counteract any variation in air currents by using a combination of wing beats and a fanned-out tail. The head is kept motionless and inclined downwards to allow the bird to scour the terrain for signs of movement by possible prey animals. Kestrels quarter the ground slowly and methodically from a height of 9 to 12 metres (30-40 feet), continually manoeuvring to turn into the wind. The strength of the wind determines the mode of hovering. A calm day requires a much greater expenditure of energy as the bird must work to maintain its position by constant wing beats. Once the bird has fixed on a possible target, it usually drops one or two levels before the final plunge, talons outstretched and wings held high above the body. The prey is either eaten on the spot or carried to a prominent point nearby. Soaring or cruise hunting tends to be used in the pursuit of birds (similar to the sparrowhawk's hunting technique) or when engaged in food piracy from other raptors, including members of its own species. The bird has been recorded successfully hunting bats in flight and, even more impressively, swifts *(Apus apus)*. Co-operative hunting has been recorded, with a pair successfully catching a long-eared bat *(Plecotus auritus)*.

In perch hunting the bird chooses a favoured perch, such as a tree, pylon or

6. The status of the kestrel populations in European countries: A, stable or increasing; B, recovering after decline; C, declining.

telegraph pole, to survey the immediate vicinity. It then drops on to the prey by means of a shallow dive. Less ground is covered, but this type of hunting is very economical on energy expenditure. Perch hunting is more often used in winter, when the birds have only themselves to support. In the Fen Country, analysis of hunting behaviour showed that kestrels perch-hunted for most of the time in winter (85 per cent as against 15 per cent); in the summer there was an equal amount of perch and flight hunting. In Sussex, the figures recorded were 64 to 36 per cent in favour of perch hunting in the period from November to January.

Kestrels may feed on carrion (hare, rabbit or gamebirds) but this is not common. Yet another method of hunting is when the kestrel forages for insects on the ground. This behaviour can look very animated and ungainly as the bird races around, lunging into vegetation to catch individual insects. The kestrel has also been seen following the plough to prey upon insects and other small invertebrates on the disturbed ground.

The food requirement of the kestrel is estimated to be about one-fifth of its body weight per day. This is about 35 to 45 grams or the equivalent of two average-sized voles or one starling. The kestrel has a better success rate catching small mammals than birds. Flight hunting is more efficient than perch hunting and is used much more during the breeding season. When the cock bird is supporting a hen and brood, it can take five to eight hours of flight hunting to catch sufficient food for the family.

There is unanimous acceptance that the short-tailed field vole is the main prey item of the kestrel in Britain and elsewhere and provides the bulk of food by weight in any year. A study in Eskdalemuir in southern Scotland showed that voles occurred in 80 per cent of pellets and accounted for 73 per cent of prey items at nests.

Along with the barn owl, the kestrel is considered to be one of the most beneficial birds to farmers because it hunts on

7. *A cock kestrel at the entrance to an urban nest site.*

8. *These pellets at a kestrel roost are composed entirely of invertebrate remains.*

9. *A hen kestrel on a typical rock-face nest ledge.*

10. *Carrion crows' nests are frequently used by kestrels and this allows them to breed in areas where cliff sites are scarce or absent.*

agricultural ground. In upland areas the cyclic nature of the vole's breeding regularly influences the density and breeding output of kestrels. Numbers of voles build up to a peak every four or five years in grassland habitats, especially newly planted forestry ground. Then the population crashes. It has been shown from ringing data that, since 1926, high densities of breeding pairs of kestrels, large clutches and large broods have been associated with vole peaks. In the late nineteenth century, when the border country of southern Scotland was very badly affected by widespread vole 'plagues', kestrels were recorded nesting colonially. The farming communities, who were losing large tracts of pasture to the voles, were delighted with the influx of kestrels and short-eared owls and their sterling work in combating the pests.

When voles are scarce, kestrel breeding density on upland grassland pasture is usually much lower and, in Norway, the kestrel may not breed at all in areas where vole numbers are very low.

Kestrels hunt over a wide range of habitats and the short-tailed field vole is not the only prey item taken. A large number of species is included in the kestrel's diet and the percentages of mammals, birds and invertebrates recorded vary enormously in different habitats. In mixed farmland in Sussex, one study showed that small mammals comprised only 50 per cent of the diet by weight, birds 46 per cent and invertebrates a seasonal maximum of 7 per cent. The bird component rose to 75 per cent in the summer.

Other mammals taken in significant numbers are the pygmy shrew *(Sorex minutus)*, common shrew *(S. araneus)*, bank vole *(Clethrionomys glareolus)* and wood mouse *(Apodemus sylvaticus)*. Mole *(Talpa europaea)*, house mouse *(Mus musculus)*, brown rat *(Rattus norvegicus)*, rabbit *(Oryctolagus cuniculus)*, water shrew *(Neomys fodicus)* and bats are taken to a much lesser extent. Weasel *(Mustela nivalis)*, red squirrel *(Sciurus vulgaris)*, grey squirrel *(S. carolinensis)* and brown hare *(Lepus capensis)* have been recorded on rare occasions.

Fledgling birds are a vital secondary source of prey providing bulk feeding for broods, especially in June, July and August. In urban areas bird prey items may surpass voles in importance in the diet. Work in Manchester, for example, showed that the house sparrow *(Passer domesticus)* dominated the diet and birds comprised 76 per cent of prey taken, compared to 22 per cent rodents and 2 per cent invertebrates. More than fifty species of birds are listed as being taken by kestrels, some quite large, like the nestlings and juveniles of waders, ducks and gulls. The majority of birds taken are smaller than the song thrush *(Turdus philomelos)* but kestrels have been known to tackle adult wood pigeons *(Columba palumbus)*, feral pigeons *(C. livia)*, hooded crows *(Corvus corone cornix)* and also green woodpeckers *(Picus viridis)*.

Although house sparrows are the commonest bird item taken, the kestrel can exact a severe toll on other species if a good feeding territory is located. In Suffolk, an analysis of kestrel pellets at one locality revealed no less than 11 bearded tit *(Panunis biarmicus)* rings. On Bardsey Island (Gwynedd), 131 rings were found in 300 pellets collected from a cock kestrel's roost. The bird's prey had included 40 wrens *(Troglodytes troglodytes)*, 49 goldcrests *(Regulus regulus)*, 20 robins *(Erithacus rubecula)*, dunnocks *(Prunella modularis)*, chiffchaffs *(Phylloscopus collybita)*, chaffinches *(Fringilla coelebs)*, a meadow pipit *(Anthus pratensis)*, a rock pipit *(Anthus spinoletta)* and a skylark *(Alauda arvensis)*. Kestrels will attend bird roosts and will also return time after time to colonies of little terns *(Sterna albifrons)* to remove nestlings. This habit of returning to good feeding areas explains the problem encountered by the rearers of gamebirds. If pens are left uncovered and a kestrel takes a chick, then it will probably come back for more. The kestrel is usually harmless to game and poultry, but individual birds will take very small pheasants *(Phasianus colchicus)*, partridges *(Perdix perdix)* and, exceptionally, red grouse *(Lagopus lagopus scoticus)*. However, young gamebirds very quickly outgrow the preferred size of prey for the kestrel.

Amphibians, lizards and invertebrates, such as ground beetles, occur frequently in the diet of kestrels but amounts vary enormously depending upon the type of habitat and the demands upon the bird at certain times of the year. In early spring, frogs and toads are added to the kestrel's staple diet of small mammals and birds, and lizards which are prone to basking are caught on sunny banks. Earthworms (Lumbricidae) are taken from March to May when they are working near the surface but in summer, when they burrow deeper, they rarely feature in the bird's diet. Earthworm remains, like bird remains, are difficult to detect in pellet debris and are probably underrecorded. Other invertebrates, which feature in impressive numerical quantity in the kestrel fare, are dung beetles (*Geotrupes* species) and ground beetles (family Carabidae), grasshoppers (family Acrididae) and numerous species of caterpillars. However, when analysed by weight, the invertebrate contribution is rarely significant. One exception was in a Cumbrian sample where insects and earthworms amounted to 87 per cent of the total number of prey animals and 27 per cent of the diet by weight. Invertebrates are taken mostly outside the breeding season. On mixed farmland the kestrel will forage extensively on cereal fields after combine harvesting in search of insects, especially ground beetles. In urban locations and upland pasture invertebrates were rarely recorded as being taken in the summer but they were taken more frequently in autumn and winter, when kestrels are supporting only themselves. The cock bird takes more insects and small birds than the hen, while juveniles are almost entirely insectivorous in the early formative days of hunting.

Although the availability of short-tailed field voles is a very important factor in determining the outcome of a breeding season, the kestrel is able to switch easily to bird prey should the need arise. Outside the breeding season the kestrel is an opportunist and will supplement the small mammal and bird content of its diet with invertebrates and amphibians whenever possible. This ability to exploit a wide variety of food sources increases the bird's chances of surviving the winter.

The breeding cycle

The duration of the kestrel's breeding season is about four months, normally April to July. This effectively restricts the bird to one brood per season, thus allowing young to be in the nest in early to mid summer, when food is plentiful. A breeding attempt may fail at the pre-laying stage. If it fails during early incubation the female may lay a second clutch. The timing of the start of the breeding cycle is also very important as early breeders tend to lay bigger clutches and rear more young, which in turn have a better chance of survival than those from later broods. Young birds from early clutches fledge sooner and thus have a longer period before the onset of bad weather. This allows them time to gain valuable experience in hunting when food is abundant.

Kestrels return to suitable nesting territories in early spring and, once a pair have become established after preliminary courtship, there is a clearly defined division of labour between male and female, typical of many birds of prey. The male takes on the role of provider for the female and later the brood, while the female spends most of her time around the nest site until well into the brood stage.

Each territory normally contains a number of potential nest sites, good shelter for roosting and access to open ground for hunting. Small but reliable feeding sites within a territory may be able to support a breeding pair. It is not uncommon for birds to return to the same territory and nest site each year. At the beginning of the season they have an almost exclusive territory, which is defended vigorously against other intruding kestrels. Greater foraging is required at this time when the preferred diet, voles, is less common. This relaxes to large overlapping territories later in the cycle, when birds regularly use communal hunting areas. Kestrels usually hunt

11. *Kestrel chicks hatching. New-born chicks weigh only 15 to 20 grams.*
12. *A kestrel chick at six days, covered in thin white down and showing the egg tooth on the upper bill.*

13. *Small birds form a major part of the diet of the young kestrels.*

14. *A brood of well grown chicks at three and a half weeks, with feathers well developed.*

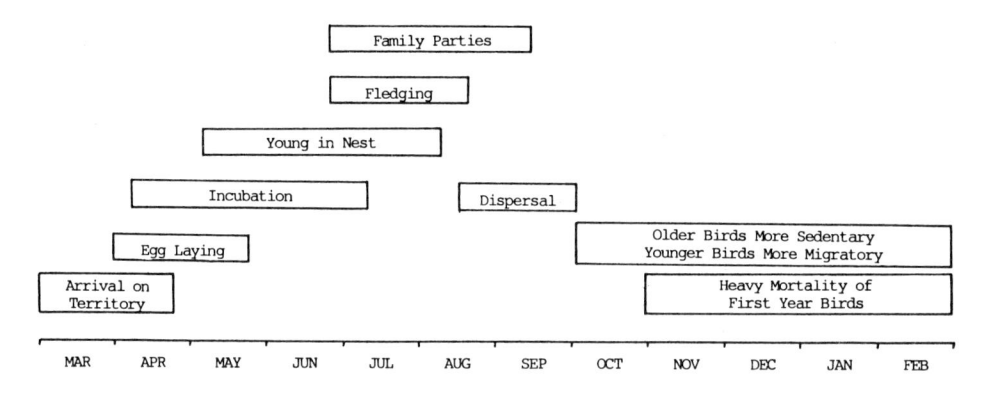

15. *The main phases in the annual cycle of the kestrel in Britain.*

within 2 km (1¼ miles) of their nest site but may travel up to 5 km (3 miles) in search of prey. They strongly defend a core of 20 to 30 metres around the nest against all potential predators. In conditions of abundant prey, however, they will tolerate close neighbours and there are numerous records of three to ten pairs on one rock face, some nesting within 10 metres of each other.

Kestrels select and compete for mates and nesting territories. Territorial fights occur and aggression between rival males or females may result in physical contact. Birds will fly directly and purposefully towards intruders and, if this does not work, then the birds buffet each other in flight, occasionally locking claws. In serious encounters the birds end up on their backs on the ground raking each other with their claws. This can result in fatalities.

Kestrels will also engage in aerial combat with crows or other birds of prey which may be attempting to nest in the vicinity. The recovery of the peregrine falcon *(Falco peregrinus)* after the pesticide problems of the 1950s and 1960s and its re-establishment on former nesting cliffs have resulted in kestrel pairs being displaced from traditional sites. Competition has also been recorded with the barn owl, tawny owl and long-eared owl.

The density of breeding kestrels is not uniform throughout Britain, nor even in one district from year to year, as the kestrel responds to different environmental conditions such as food and nest-site availability. This is further complicated by the fact that nests are often clumped when suitable nest sites are scarce over a wide area. Thus in upland districts of southern Scotland kestrels nest in concentrations in the valleys while large areas of adjacent hill ground have few nests. In the relatively uniform farmland habitats in eastern England clumping is less obvious but nests are still unevenly distributed. In changing landscapes, such as newly afforested ground, the number of pairs nesting in traditional sites may well be swollen by pairs responding to new food sources and for many years there may be high densities. When the tree canopy closes the density often reverts to the earlier pattern. By comparison, in East Anglia small stable sedentary populations exist.

Aerial displays, often accompanied by high-pitched calling, are an important part of courtship. These involve soaring together above the prospective nest site, chasing each other and spectacular mock attacks. If the female is perched, the male will dive at her, pulling away at the last moment and soaring up to repeat the manoeuvre. Touching claws in mid flight has also been noted. Display flights often end with one of the birds flying to the nest site with wings raised high above its body. Although they are generally monogamous, there are several records of polygamous behaviour.

The kestrel, like most falcons, does not build a 'nest' and often lays its eggs on a ledge on a rock face. By using other birds' nests, such as the stick platform of the carrion crow *(Corvus corone corone)*, ledges on buildings or holes in trees, the kestrel has been able to breed in places where there are no rock faces.

The nest site is scraped out by the hen using leg and chest movements to shape a rough bowl for the eggs. The build-up of pellets and other debris soon gives the semblance of a lined nest. Kestrels nest on the ground among heather in Orkney, where ground predators are absent, but on mainland Britain this is a rare occurrence.

The most demanding stages in the kestrel breeding cycle occur before and during egg laying, when both birds need to expend a lot of energy. For at least a week before the first egg is laid in the chosen scrape, the female becomes very inactive, spending much of her time in the vicinity of the nest site. While she is in this lethargic state, the male hunts and brings food to her.

Eggs are laid in the morning at two-day intervals. The timing of the laying varies from season to season depending upon prevailing environmental conditions. Birds lay later in cold wet springs and earlier when conditions are warm and dry, the range being from mid March to the beginning of June. Those in northern Britain tend to nest ten days later than their counterparts in the south, although there are always exceptions to this.

The eggs are broad and oval and measure on average 39 by 31 mm. The buff-white ground colour is invariably marked by heavy red-brown speckling. Even within a clutch, the colour variation can be striking. Clutch sizes range from one to seven eggs, but most birds lay between four and six. Again, there is a regional variation, with birds in the north laying slightly larger clutches.

Incubation lasts 27 to 29 days for each egg and this is undertaken primarily by the hen. She normally starts incubating after the third egg is laid. During the incubation period she begins to moult, but despite the discarded feathers the nest site remains relatively unobtrusive. Attention is drawn to the nest site only when the area is defended against intruders or when food is being brought in. The male arrives with food and calls to the female, who responds by calling before coming off the eggs to receive the prey item. The male often covers the eggs for a while until the hen returns. Towards the end of incubation the cock bird may cache a supply of food in anticipation of the brood hatching.

The chicks can be heard tapping and cheeping inside the eggs even before they begin the process of chipping their way out, about 24 to 28 hours before hatching. They emerge with the help of the egg tooth, wet and exhausted, barely able to raise their heads. The hen assists the young out of the egg if necessary and removes the shells from the nest. A clutch of five normally takes three to five days to hatch and each young bird weighs only 15 to 20 grams. This is the second time of severe pressure in the breeding cycle when, following the relatively easy spell during incubation, the pair move into a much more demanding phase. The cock bird in particular has to accelerate food production from the equivalent of four voles per day to as many as 28. Chicks gain weight slowly at first, then increase rapidly to around 280 grams for females and 250 grams for males at about 21 days. There is then a slight weight loss before they leave the nest.

The first week of the brood period is probably the time when the young are most vulnerable. They are helpless, unable to stand and have their eyes closed for the first few days. They are covered in a thin white down and are in need of almost constant brooding and attention from the hen. She rarely leaves the vicinity of the nest site except to pick up food from the incoming male. The food item is invariably decapitated and, holding it down with her claws, she tears off small pieces of meat and proffers them gently to the brood. Once satisfied, the young slump back into the prone position. Even at this stage droppings are deposited over the rim of the scrape. If young are lost through natural causes it is usually in the first week, and it is often

16. *The cock bird will incubate the eggs for short periods when the hen is away feeding.*

17. *It is very unusual for the cock bird to brood the newly hatched chicks.*

18. *The hen kestrel is an attentive parent and will retrieve young which wander from the nest.*

19. *When the chicks are over two weeks old the cock bird is allowed into the nest site to drop off food. He rarely stays for more than a few seconds.*

the last chick to hatch which dies.

After the first week a second, thicker and longer down layer develops, buff-grey above and paler below. The hen still feeds the chicks but small prey is eaten whole, though not without great effort. She still protects them from the elements, mantling them to shield them from excessive sun and rain, and will retrieve any wanderers. Rarely is the male allowed into the nest. At the beginning of the third week the first feathers begin to appear on the wings and tail, and activity in the nest increases. Pestered incessantly while at the nest, the female confines her visits to feeding times but does not leave the site unattended. The male now comes in and helps to feed and by about twenty days the chicks are capable of tearing food and feeding themselves competently.

Ever alert to the calls of the adults, the young respond to alarm calls by crouching low in the nest and remaining motionless until the danger is past. When adults approach with food they jostle for position and grab for the prey item. Usually one chick is successful in grabbing the food, which is quickly mantled. The chick turns its back on the rest and shields the item with outstretched wings. Between feeds the young doze, flap their wings or practise foot stabbing on pieces of debris in the nest. The nest itself is now more obvious due to the accumulation of droppings, the remains of prey and moulted down feathers. Concealment is not so important now as the brood are well able to defend themselves by lying on their backs and raking any intruder with their sharp claws.

In the last week, the young still have tufts of down on their heads and back but the feathers are well formed. The male continues to provide most of the food but the female spends more time away from the immediate vicinity of the nest hunting. Food is dropped in at the nest and the adults rarely spend more than a few seconds on site. The young are now very aware of the environs of the nest and spend a lot of time staring around, probably familiarising themselves with their immediate surroundings. Near

20. *Kestrels ringed in Fenno-Scandinavia and recovered in Britain.*

fledging, if the site allows, they begin to move out of the nest on to nearby branches and ledges, returning to the safety of the base to feed and roost. The males leave slightly earlier, at 27 to 30 days, compared to the females' 29 to 32 days, though there is considerable variation.

The fledging period is another of the stress points in the cycle and accidents can happen to the inexperienced birds. They gradually drift from the nest and stay in its vicinity for the first two weeks. At least a month is spent in the company of the adults, learning to hunt. They soon learn to hover, and they catch prey from the adults in the air. Their first kill, usually of an invertebrate, is made after ten days. Much of their early hunting is done from a perch. Adults bring in food regularly at first, but this is reduced gradually until the juveniles are hunting for themselves. Dispersal from the family group and the home territory takes place after six to seven weeks.

The overall breeding success of the kestrel in Britain is high. The average clutch size of 4.7 can be as high as 5.5 in years when voles are plentiful and many pairs rear a full brood from clutches of six eggs. Hatching rates are usually around 75 per cent and, once the young hatch, the survival rate is excellent. Although the failure rate does vary annually, the general consensus is that 70 to 80 per cent of pairs usually rear at least one young. The most vulnerable period is undoubtedly the pre-laying and clutch stages, when desertion, due to adverse weather conditions, insufficient prey, human interference or competition for nest sites from other raptors, accounts for the majority of failures. Human interference is a major problem in urban areas where nests are accessible.

Breeding numbers and performance are usually higher in years when warm dry springs affect the density and availability of voles. Heavy rain affects both hunting efficiency and prey availability and therefore the amount of food the male is able to provide for the pair. Surface activity of voles diminishes when it rains and during heavy rain kestrels are reluctant to hunt. Severe weather can also destroy nest sites and cause desertion. In warm dry springs kestrels tend to breed earlier, lay larger clutches and rear more young.

Migration and mortality

The family parties break up in late summer and the young birds seem to wander initially in any direction. If the birds do migrate, they do so in a southerly direction. The kestrel is nomadic by nature but it is generally accepted that after the first year the majority of kestrels are relatively sedentary. There is a general displacement from north to south. Considering conditions in winter in the northern and eastern margins of the kestrel's range in Europe, it is hardly surprising that they move out as the food supply must be extremely limited for a small-mammal hunter. Ringing recoveries and data from North Sea oil installations confirm the autumn movement of a considerable number of kestrels from Fenno-Scandinavia to Britain. Juvenile kestrels from Scotland and the north of England move to the south of England and the northern fringes of the continent of Europe. On average, juveniles move further south than adults and northern birds further than those from southern England. Ireland is a subsidiary wintering area for kestrels from the north of England and Scotland. Ringing recoveries have shown that juveniles from the continent of Europe move across to Africa, many of them crossing the Sahara Desert. Birds have travelled from the Netherlands to Mauritania, from Switzerland to Libya, from Czechoslovakia to Ghana and from East Germany to Nigeria. So far, no British kestrel has been known to travel to Africa, though some birds born in the south of England have been recovered in southern Spain.

The main movements of kestrels begin in August on the northern edge of the range and continue throughout September and October in Europe. The southern movement reaches Africa by early October and the equator by the middle of the

21. *A hen kestrel with her young at a cliff site.*

22. *Sixty per cent of recently fledged kestrels fail to survive their first winter.*

same month. On migration the kestrels fly higher than in normal flight and are gregarious, being seen in diffuse flocks of several hundreds, often mixed with lesser kestrels and red-footed falcons *(Falco vespertinus)*. The homeward journey of British birds from Europe begins in February, with a peak in March. The migration occurs on wide fronts with concentrations at narrow sea crossings. There is evidence that birds return to the area of the country where they were reared, but not specifically to the natal site.

Data from ringing recoveries have shown that the mortality rate of kestrels in their first year is very high. 60 to 65 per cent die in their first year, many of exhaustion and starvation in November and December, when they are unable to cope with difficult hunting conditions at the onset of severe winter weather. Early-hatched young have a better chance of surviving than those from later broods, presumably having had the advantage of more time to build up body reserves and having gained more experience in hunting. Mortality is slightly less over periods when vole numbers are on the increase than at times when voles are declining. The average life span of a kestrel has been calculated at 1.3 years, but some have lived well into their teens. Fourteen years and five months is the British record so far, but a Swiss bird reached the impressive age of seventeen years. The mortality rate for birds in their second year has been estimated, again from ringing recoveries, at 47 per cent, and 34 per cent for subsequent years.

Causes of death can be categorised under four main headings: accidental injury, human persecution or interference, predation and environmental conditions. Although not as accident-prone as the dashing sparrowhawk or low-flying merlin *(Falco columbarius)*, many kestrels are involved in fatal collisions each year. Because they hunt at a height of 7 to 10 metres (20 to 30 feet), overhead wires are a hazard. The volume of traffic on Britain's roads has increased dramatically since the 1960s and there has been a corresponding increase in kestrel deaths on roads. Excellent hunting opportunities have been offered by wide grass verges, thus increasing the likelihood of collisions with vehicles. Other types of accidental death recorded for the kestrel are flying into buildings (presumably while chasing prey) and drowning. One unfortunate bird was oiled by fulmars *(Fulmarus glacialis)* in Orkney.

Persecution by man is still a major cause for concern despite full legal protection for this species. Kestrels are very vulnerable to shooting during the breeding season, especially when they use crows' nests. Hovering as a method of hunting also makes them an easier target than many other raptors. The kestrel does not seem to suffer from poisoning as badly as does the buzzard and instances of pesticide poisoning have been greatly reduced since the 1950s and 1960s.

Predation by other species is not a significant cause of mortality in the kestrel population but it does happen. There are several recorded instances of kestrels being killed by peregrine falcons and even golden eagles *(Aquila chrysaetos)*. One ringing recovery was of a kestrel killed at a French Air Force base by a trained peregrine, which was carrying out its duties as a bird scarer. On the recovery form, the cause of death was entered as 'public safety'. Kestrels have also been recorded as the prey of sparrowhawk, goshawk and tawny owl. Predation by mammals such as foxes has been recorded, but only on rare occasions, and probably most cases relate to injured birds.

Prolonged spells of severe weather, either continuous rain or snow cover, can be fatal even for experienced birds, as the 1962-3 winter proved. Weakened birds are more susceptible to disease and analysis of corpses at Monkswood Experimental Station has shown that kestrels are liable to catch Newcastle disease and also suffer from tuberculosis, which is probably the most commonly recorded disease of wild birds of prey.

The future

Numerically, kestrels make up two-thirds of Britain's birds of prey. While other species have struggled to cope with man's impact on the environment since the Second World War, kestrel numbers have increased. The kestrel's lifestyle has certain key elements which enable it as a species to respond quickly and positively to any major environmental changes.

As a partial migrant with nomadic tendencies, it is capable of utilising favourable conditions such as an increased food supply in a district. This mobility, allied to reasonable tolerance of near neighbours, often results in almost colonial breeding at times. They can also search for suitable vacant territories over a wide area in spring and move great distances to suitable feeding areas in winter, unlike some sedentary species.

In general, kestrels have relatively short lives but this is more than compensated for by a high reproductive rate and the early maturity of young birds. Large clutches, good hatching rates and brood survival combine to ensure a more than adequate replacement for adult mortality. In addition, if the population crashes for some reason, as in the pesticide era, it has the potential to recover quickly. Kestrels are also able to breed in their first year and the presence of a floating reservoir of birds capable of recruitment into the breeding population, if conditions are favourable, is an obvious advantage.

The five-month breeding cycle is reasonably short, which means that the adults and young are vulnerable at the nest site for a much shorter period than some of their larger counterparts. The golden eagle's breeding cycle, for example, can take up most of the year and they may not even be able to breed annually. The osprey takes nearly ninety days from egg to fledging, compared to sixty for the kestrel. If a kestrel clutch is lost at an early stage, the cycle can be restarted, which again is not possible in larger species because of the time factor.

Another great advantage is the lack of specialisation in the kestrel's lifestyle, a point often masked as many people see the bird only as a hovering falcon. However, there is diversity in every aspect of its lifestyle. The only major habitats kestrels avoid are dense forest and water. Even so, there have been records of kestrels hunting successfully in aquatic habitats, such as reservoirs and streams, taking live fish. The kestrel is at home from coastline to hilltop as long as the terrain is open. It is particularly well adapted to urban environments. Buildings provide surrogate cliffs, and playing fields, parks, gardens and railway lines are good substitutes for rough grassland pasture. During the period 1963-73, when the British population of kestrels increased fivefold, the diversity of nesting habitats quadrupled.

The availability of food and the existence of suitable nest sites are probably the most important factors in determining the density of birds of prey in an area. For the kestrel, the latter factor is less important because it can use an impressive range of sites. Not being a nest builder, it relies heavily on substitutes for cliff ledges, but this is no impediment as buildings or other man-made structures are used. The German name for the kestrel, *Turmfalke* (tower falcon), is testimony to this habit in central Europe. The old or disused nests of ravens *(Corvus corax)*, carrion crows, herons *(Ardea cinerea)*, magpies *(Pica pica)* and sparrowhawks are equally acceptable. The role of the carrion crow cannot be overstressed as in upland areas their stick nests are used frequently by kestrels. Holes in trees are used, especially in the south-east of England, and the hurricane damage of 1987 combined with the previous loss of nesting holes due to Dutch elm disease could pose a problem in this part of Britain. The kestrel does take readily to nest-boxes and they have been used successfully in the Polders of Holland to encourage kestrels to breed in areas where natural sites are scarce or absent. Unusual nest sites have included window boxes in high-rise flats and even an aeroplane at Gatwick Airport.

The subject of food and hunting is a critical one and further illustrates the point about lack of specialisation. Exploiting different prey populations and employing different hunting techniques gives the opportunist kestrel more options. The ability to switch from one food source to another when conditions change can make the difference between surviving the winter and not, or between rearing a brood and failing to produce.

The speed at which the kestrel is able to react positively to changes in the environment and the resourcefulness of the bird are quite remarkable. Colonisation of urban locations, triggered by the sudden availability of nest sites and hunting areas in bombed cities, spread quickly as figures from London show. In 1898 W. H. Hudson commented that it was highly unlikely that kestrels would ever return to London. However, in 1931 a pair nested in Hammersmith and by 1950 five pairs were breeding in the 10 square miles (26 sq km) of central London. In 1967 a survey carried out by the London Natural History Society revealed 98 definite, 13 probable and 31 possible breeding pairs within a 20 mile (32 km) radius of St Paul's Cathedral. Similarly in Birmingham the kestrel breeding numbers began to build up in 1950, reaching a minimum of 45 territories in 1976. Many of the nest sites in urban locations are in commercial and industrial buildings or churches, often inaccessible to the general public.

Another good example of a rapid change, this time in nest-site preference, comes from the Orkney Islands. In 1945 the late Edward Balfour, the Royal Society for the Protection of Birds warden, found a kestrel nesting on the ground in a strip of luxuriant heather, having abandoned the traditional cliff site nearby. This was a new departure as kestrel pairs normally nested on the abundant sea cliffs and there was no previous knowledge of ground nests on the islands. Follow-up work in subsequent years confirmed a gradual increase in ground-nesting birds, matched with an increase in the diversity of nest sites used — under low banks, in rabbit burrows and in peaty ground. By 1955 63 definite nest sites had been located on mainland Orkney, nineteen of them ground nests, including seven in rabbit holes. Because of the absence of ground predators on the island, there was minimal risk compared to mainland British pairs. The shelduck *(Tadorna tadorna)* was the keenest competitor for nest sites. In the short space of a decade, kestrels seemed to have moved from conventional cliff nesting and its attendant problems to the comparative safety of sites in deep cover and the reduced chance of young falling out of the nest.

Afforestation of mainly upland localities in Britain on a huge scale began in the mid 1960s and peaked in the late 1970s. Thousands of acres of upland moorland and sheep pasture were fenced, fertilised and planted with monoculture conifers, radically altering the landscape but, in the short term, providing ideal feeding conditions for the kestrel, short-eared owl and hen harrier. The exclusion of sheep and the upgrading of the grassland provided ideal habitats for short-tailed field voles. Provided that nest sites were available, the density of kestrels in these new plantations was extremely high. Although the scale of planting has decreased or levelled off in many areas, the second-generation plantings will, it is hoped, provide continuity as will better designed forests with more planned open space.

There is little doubt that, allied to the bird's mobility, breeding output, catholic lifestyle and ability to respond quickly to changes, its relationship with man has been a vital factor in the bird's success. Much of this success is due to the fact that it has virtually no conflicts with traditional countryside practices. Even in game-rearing circles, the kestrel is regarded on the whole as being reasonably harmless and is not persecuted as much as the sparrowhawk, peregrine falcon and hen harrier.

The other great bonus for the kestrel is that, being both common and widespread, it is kept in the public eye and this very familiarity has bred affection. The kestrel is one of the best known and most popular birds in Britain and this manifests itself in all sorts of ways. Kestrels breeding in urban locations are often given devoted protection by the people who live or work nearby. In the Gatwick Airport incident already mentioned the airport workers refused to disturb the kestrel pair which were nesting on the wing structure of an old Comet used for training. They returned to a normal routine only after the pair had reared five chicks. Unusual sites chosen by kestrels are regularly featured by the media and its angular hovering outline has been a delight to signwriters. As a symbol, the kestrel appears in all sorts of guises: Kestrel Press, Kestrel Marine, Kestrel Tours, Kestrel Lager, and on pub signs. As the symbol of the junior branch of the RSPB, the Young Ornithologists' Club, the kestrel is known to thousands of children. On the debit side, in the 1970s there was an unprecedented rise in the number of kestrel chicks taken by would-be young falconers, following the successful film *Kes*, but this has receded as a problem. The loss of clutches to egg-collecting children is still prevalent despite the protective legislature and is a major educational challenge.

The kestrel population is stable at present and in many areas is at optimum density but, being at the top of the food chain, it is still vulnerable to major environmental problems. Loss of habitat and persecution do not seem to affect the kestrel as much as other species such as the merlin or golden eagle, but its future will depend largely upon how the countryside is managed or mismanaged — and man's prevailing attitude towards wildlife. The international kestrel is no respecter of boundaries and could easily be affected by conditions well away from their breeding areas. However, the unpredictable, opportunist kestrel is undoubtedly the best equipped of our birds of prey to survive the twentieth century and beyond.

Further reading

Bijleveld, M. *Birds of Prey in Europe*. Macmillan Press, 1974.
Brown, L., and Amadon, D. *Eagles, Hawks and Falcons of the World*, volume 2. Country Life Books, 1968.
Brown, L. *British Birds of Prey*. Collins, 1976.
Cramp, S., and Simmons, K. E. L. (editors). *Handbook of the Birds of Europe, the Middle East and North Africa*, volume 2. Oxford University Press, 1980.
Newton, I. *Population Ecology of Raptors*. T. and A. D. Poyser, 1979.

ACKNOWLEDGEMENTS
The author wishes to thank Dr J. Jackson, Miss D. Mackinnon and Mrs W. Hollingworth for help in preparing the text. Photographs are acknowledged as follows: Abraham Cardwell and Aquilla Photographics, 7; David Clugston, 5; Jim Young, 9 and 14. The acknowledgements for line drawings are: Deirdre Mackinnon, 6, 15 and 20; Deirdre Mackinnon and the British Trust for Ornithology, 2; T. and A. D. Poyser Ltd, 3. The remaining photographs are by the author.